Safe and Sound

A Common Sense Approach to Protecting Yourself and Your Property Against Crime

CONTENTS

◆

INTRODUCTION

It used to be that commonplace crime was more or less an inner-city problem.

Today, doors that were once left unlocked even in small towns must now be bolted shut. In communities across the country, walking at night is considered too risky.

Muggings, car theft, drugs, burglary, shootings, random violence and other serious crime now affect the corporate executive as well as farmer, the senior citizen as well as the grade school student.

Mayberry, the fictitious southern town where crime mainly consisted of an occasional jaywalker or litterbug, is now only a dusty TV rerun. A bit of wishful nostalgia.

It seems no one is immune from crime.

One of the biggest problems about crime is people's fear of it.

Once you learn how to protect yourself—and your property—you no longer are paralyzed by fear. And you can combat crime.

This booklet arms you with knowledge. It offers practical steps you can take in your daily life to guard you, your family and your property against crime.

Each section deals with a different topic—from personal safety to home security to travel tips.

SAFE AND SOUND is your personal guide to peace of mind. It's one way of helping to ensure that you, your family and your property don't become another crime statistic.

◆

PROTECTION AGAINST ASSAULT

Most crimes against people happen on the streets. So it's important that you are street smart. Wherever you are—in a parking lot, on a sidewalk, in a public hallway—stay alert to what's going on around you.

Show confidence through your mannerisms. Send the message that you're calm and confident, and that you know where you're going.

It's important, too, that you trust your instincts. If something about your surroundings makes you feel nervous or uncomfortable, leave the area.

You spend most of your life at home and at work. So take some time to know the areas. Check out what stores and restaurants are open at night. Find out the locations of the public phones, and the police and fire stations.

If You're Walking

Don't carry a lot of money.
Try not to carry more money than you can afford to lose. If you simply have no choice, women should try to avoid putting the money in their purses. An inside coat pocket is safer. Men should put their wallets in an inside coat or front pants pocket.

Avoid short-cuts.
Stick to streets that are well-lighted and well-traveled.

Wear proper clothes.
Expensive clothes and jewelry are invitations to potential trouble. Be sure that whatever you wear, your clothes and shoes don't restrict your movements.

Have your key ready.
Make sure you have your key in your hand before you reach the door of your home, car or office.

If you're being followed, let your pursuer know that you know it.
Cross the street. Change directions. Then go straight for help—whether it's an open restaurant, a lighted house, a telephone or the police.

At night, avoid curbs, doorways and shrubbery.
They are potential ambush points for you or your belongings. Use the middle of the sidewalk. Vary your route if you walk at night regularly.

If you're working late, get an escort.
Ask a security guard or friend to walk with you to your car or transit stop.

If You're Driving

Keep your car in good running condition.
And make sure there's enough gas to get you where you're going and back.

Keep windows rolled up and doors locked.
Check the inside of your vehicle before you get in.

If you're being followed, don't head home—especially if no one else is home.
Indicate to the pursuer you know you're being followed. Speed up. Slow down. Change directions. Then go straight for help—to the nearest busy, brightly lighted place.

Consider a cellular phone.
It tells a would-be pursuer you have instant access to help. It also offers you a safeguard during car breakdowns, when you can be vulnerable to attackers.

Avoid parking in isolated areas.
Enclosed and underground parking garages require special vigilance.

Don't pick up hitchhikers.
And don't be a hitchhiker yourself.

PROTECTION AGAINST ASSAULT

If You're on a Bus or Subway

Use busy stops.
And make sure they are well-lighted.

Stay alert.
Don't doze or daydream.

Don't accept harassment.
Loudly say, "Leave me alone!" If that doesn't work, hit the emergency device.

Watch who gets off with you.
If you feel uneasy, get back on the bus or train if possible. Otherwise, walk directly to a place where there are other people.

If You're Shopping

Avoid paying for large purchases with cash.
It makes you a more likely target for would-be attackers.

If possible, have your packages delivered.
It reduces the risk of being assaulted on the street by someone trying to grab your bags.

Store packages in your trunk.
Avoid placing them in your back seat. Try to make your major purchases the last ones before going home.

Park your car near higher traffic areas.
This is especially helpful if parking in a shopping center lot. Park near a source of light if shopping at night. Avoid parking near concealing shrubbery.

Look inside your car before you get in.
Then, lock your doors when you get inside. Be wary of strangers who approach you in a lot.

Have your door key ready before you get to your front door.
Lock the door as soon as you are inside.

If You're Using an Automated Teller Machine

Use an active location during daylight hours.

If using an ATM at night, find one that has a secured, well-lighted enclosed lobby area. It's your best protection against robbery.

Go with someone.
There's safety in numbers.

Be cautious.
Look around for suspicious people. Wait until any loiterers leave or find another ATM.

Don't waste time.
Have your card ready, complete your transaction and leave as soon as possible. Don't flash cash around. Put it away.

Make sure you're not being followed as you drive away.
ATM robbers have been known to follow their victims and attack them as they get out of their cars.

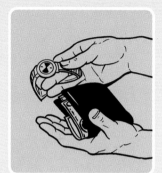

If You're Confronted

Give up your valuables.
Try to remain calm and obey all commands.

Avoid letting the attacker move you to another place.
An alley, doorway or a car are danger areas.

If you're attacked, act fast.
Your best defense is to scream and run away—not to fight. Chances are the robber is better equipped for street fighting than you are.

Report the incident to the police.
Be as accurate as you can. It can help prevent others from being victims.

Special Precautions Against Rape

Many of the suggestions listed on the previous pages also apply to potential rape situations. Consider these additional safeguards:

Use good judgment.
Don't let alcohol or other drugs cloud your common sense.

Use dead-bolt locks on windows and doors.
Install a peephole in exterior doors and keep entrances well-lighted.

Don't open doors to strangers.
If the person needs to make a call, you make it. Check identification of sales or service people before letting them in. Phone for verification.

Know your neighbors.
It helps if you need a place to go or someone to call if you're concerned or scared.

If you come home and see a door or window inexplicably open, don't go inside.
Call the police from a public phone or neighbor's home.

Be careful if someone in a car asks for help.
Keep your distance from the car. Don't agree to go with them.

If your car breaks down, use caution.
Lift the hood. Use flares or a "Call Police" banner. Lock the doors and turn on flashers. If someone stops, roll the window down slightly and ask the person to call the police.

Safe and Sound

Handling Attempted Rape

There are no right or wrong answers to handling an actual
rape attack. Each situation is different, depending on your
physical and emotional state—and the rapist's. Surviving is
the goal.

Stall for time.
Talk. Figure out your options.

**If the rapist is armed, you may
have little choice but to submit.**
Do whatever it takes to survive.

If you fight, hit hard and fast.
Be effective. Target the eyes and groin. Escape as soon as
possible. You might want to consider professional self-
defense training.

Try to escape.
Be rude. Scream. Make noises to discourage the attacker
from following.

Preventing Attempted Date Rape

As a woman, you can:

Let your date know your limits.
Keep communications open as any relationship develops. Don't take anything for granted.

Keep your senses clear.
Don't let alcohol or other drugs interfere with your judgment.

Trust your gut feelings.
If the way he acts makes you nervous, get out.

Check out a first date with friends.
Insist on going to a public place like a movie or restaurant. Carry money for a phone call and a taxi. Or take your own car.

Avoid strangers.
Don't leave a party or other social event with someone you just met or hardly know.

Be wary of men with "attitudes."
Avoid men around you who put you down or try to control how you dress or your choice of friends.

As a man, you can:

Accept a woman's decision.
When she says "no," don't challenge her.

Stay sharp.
Don't cloud your judgment with alcohol or other drugs.

Check your stereotypes.
Do they affect your attitudes toward women?

Recognize the consequences.
Forcing a woman to have sex is rape, a violent crime with serious consequences.

Check your feelings.
If you have feelings of violence or aggression against women, seek counseling or a support group.

If Rape Occurs

Report it!
Don't isolate yourself. Call the police, a friend or rape crisis center. Don't ignore it. The sooner you tell, the greater the chances the rapist will be caught. If it's a rape by someone you know, it is a violation of both your body and your trust.

Preserve all physical evidence.
Don't shower, wash, douche, change your clothes or throw any clothes away.

Seek medical care.
Go to a hospital emergency room or your own doctor immediately. Take a friend or family member with you.

Get counseling.
Help is available for the emotional trauma that comes with rape. It helps to talk with someone about the rape, whether it occurred last night or years ago. Remember, rape is not your fault; you are an innocent victim.

HOME SECURITY

More than two million homes will be burglarized this year. Average theft: nearly $1,300.

Most burglars will work no longer than a minute or two to get into a home. So, the more difficult you make it for thieves to enter your home, the less likely your risk of a break-in.

Look over your home. Ask yourself: If you are locked out of your home, can you get in? If you can, so can a burglar.

Spending a little time and money now to strengthen your home's doors, locks, windows and exterior can reduce your risk of being burglarized—or assaulted.

◆

Check Your Locks

Always use your locks.

In more than 40 percent of residential burglaries, the thieves just walked through an unlocked door or crawled through an unlocked window.

All exterior doors should have dead-bolt locks.

If your doors have key-in-the-knob locks, add deadbolts to them. The deadbolts should have a throw bolt that extends at least 1 inch when locked. Be sure that screws for the lock are anchored in solid wood or metal.

Consider "double-cylinder" deadbolts.

They require a key for both sides of the door. They work especially well for doors that have glass close to the lock. Intruders can't break the glass and unlock the door by reaching through. Some jurisdictions don't allow these locks. Check with your local police or building code authorities. If you use one of these locks, keep a key nearby—but at least 40 inches from the door.

Secure sliding glass doors.

Try these options:

1. Special locks are available commercially.

2. Use a broomstick or wood dowel in the track to jam the door.

3. Insert screws along the upper track of the door, secured to the frame. Leave enough room for the door to slide, but not enough space for the door to be lifted out.

Try a "police lock."

It works best on basement, rear and apartment doors. It's a metal bar bracketed against the inside of the door at an angle. The bar slides into a small hole in the floor.

Don't hide keys outside.

Burglars know all the hiding places. Give an extra key to a neighbor you trust.

Rekey the locks.

If you've just moved into a new house or apartment, this expense can save you the pain and cost of a burglary.

Check Your Windows

Don't rely on thumb-turn locks.
They can be easily opened through a broken pane.

Lock double-hung windows.
There are a couple of ways to lock them:

1. Use a special dead-bolt lock found in hardware stores. Some jurisdictions have restrictions on these locks. Check with your police before using them.

2. Slide a bolt or nail through a hole drilled at a downward angle in each top corner of the inside sash and part way through the outside sash.

Use grilles or grates for louvered windows.
These devices should be used for any especially vulnerable window. Make sure there is a quick release feature for emergency exits and that all family members know how to use them. Or, apply a two-part epoxy resin to each pane of glass to prevent easy removal.

Check Your Doors

Make sure they're solid.
Outside doors—including the one between your house and garage—should be solid wood or 1 3/4-inch metal.

Make sure they fit.
Doors should fit snugly in their frames. If not, buy some metal weather stripping to help make a tight fit.

Check where the hinges are located.
The hinge pins should be strong and on the inside. Consider non-removable or hidden pins.

Make sure the "strike" is properly installed.
The strike is the metal plate in which the latch rests. It should be installed with 2 1/2- or 3-inch screws. If not possible, use an extra-long strike plate.

Install a wide-angle viewer or peephole.
It helps you see who is on the outside without opening the door. A short chain between the door and jam can be easily broken.

Check the Outside

Prune trees and shrubbery around windows.

And make sure ladders are properly stored to prevent easy access to upper floor windows.

Keep your yard well-maintained.

Store ladders and tools in your garage or basement when not in use.

Light your yard.

Porches, entrances and yards should be well-lighted. Place some lights out of reach from the ground so bulbs can't be removed or broken. Aim floodlights away from your house so you can see if anyone is coming. Place lights at opposite corners to eliminate dark areas. Consider timers for outside lights and motion detectors.

Keep your neighborhood in good shape.

Dark alleys, broken street lights, litter, graffiti and abandoned cars attract crime. Work with your neighborhood and local officials to organize clean-up days.

Deadbolt or padlock all doors to your detached garage and exterior buildings.

Look for sturdy padlocks that don't release the key until they are locked. They should have a 3/8-inch shackle. The hasp should be secured with bolts mounted on a metal plate. The bolts should be hidden when the padlock is locked.

Let's Be Careful Out There...

Burglars don't like surprises. If they pick a home that's occupied, or are startled by someone coming home, a dangerous situation could occur.

If you see signs of a break-in, don't go in.

A slit screen, broken window or door inexplicably ajar are warning signs. Call the police from a neighbor's house or a public phone.

If you hear a break-in happening, leave safely if you can.

Then, call the police and wait for them to come. Otherwise, lock yourself in a room and call. If the intruder is in the room, pretend to be asleep.

Think carefully about buying a firearm.

Guns can be stolen or captured and used on you or the police. If you own a gun, lock it up and learn how to use it safely.

Checklist for Apartments

Apartment

☐ Entry doors have dead-bolt locks and peepholes.

☐ Sliding glass door has locking metal bar or rod in track so it can't be opened and pins in the overhead frame so it can't be lifted out.

☐ Landlord or building manager closely controls all access keys.

TIP: Leave a radio or TV playing, or a light on while you're gone. Always tell neighbors and the building manager when you leave for extended periods of time.

Building

☐ There is positive control over who enters and leaves the building.

☐ Walkways, entrances, elevators, hallways, laundry rooms and other areas are well-lighted 24 hours a day.

☐ Fire stairs are locked from the stairwell side above the ground floor, so you can exit but no one can enter.

☐ Mailboxes have good locks and are in well-traveled, well-lighted areas.

☐ Interior and exteriors are well-maintained.

Neighbors

☐ You know your neighbors.

☐ You belong to an Apartment Watch group.

☐ You've considered a tenant patrol that watches for crime around the building, provides escort services, monitors comings and goings in the lobby, etc.

☐ You work with the landlord to sponsor social events for tenants, including children and teens.

SECURITY WHEN YOU'RE AWAY FROM HOME

In the time it takes you to read this sentence, another burglary will happen in the U.S. That statistic from the Federal Bureau of Investigation emphasizes the need to protect your property.

That's especially true when you're not home to protect it.

This section of SAFE AND SOUND provides tips on how to protect your home when you're away.

It also arms you with information about how to protect yourself and your belongings when you travel.

◆

Home Security When You're Away

Use light timers.

Use the timers in several rooms. Use logical lighting patterns: on in the living room at dusk; on in the bedroom when you'd normally prepare for bed, etc. Putting a radio on a timer is another good idea.

Leave shades and blinds in normal positions.

It helps make the house look occupied.

Stop mail and newspaper deliveries.

Have the post office hold your mail. Call the newspaper to stop delivery.

Ask a trusted neighbor to help.

Your neighbor can watch over the house, tend the yard and pick up deliveries. Give this person a spare key. Don't hide it around your home.

Update your home inventory.

List things like TVs, jewelry, silver, camcorders and computers. Take photos or videos of the items. List their ID numbers. Your local police may have information about engraving your valuables.

Lock your windows and doors before you go.

Make sure the locks are working properly.

Are alarms a good idea?

You may want to consider an alarm system if you have many valuables in your home, if you live in an isolated area, or if your neighborhood has a history of break-ins.

Check out the options.

Many different electronic alarms and security devices are available on the market. Information sources include your police department, public library or Better Business Bureau.

Look for an established company.

Check references before signing a contract.

Learn how to use your system properly.

Neighbors will ignore the alarm if it is continually set off. And, you may be fined under local or state anti-false alarm laws.

Don't let your answering machine be a tip-off.

Never leave a message on your answering machine that indicates you may be away from home.

DON'T SAY: "I'm not at home now."

DO SAY: "I'm not available right now. Please leave a message."

DON'T SAY: "I'm on vacation this week."

DO SAY: "Thanks for calling. Please leave your name and number and I'll get back to you."

Personal Security When You're Away

Before you leave:
Plan ahead.
If you're traveling by car, know the route you're taking. Check the car's tires, belts and fluids before you leave.

Leave important information with a friend.
In case you need to replace them, leave a list of the numbers of your driver's license, passport, credit cards and traveler's checks with a trusted friend.

Create the illusion you're home.
Use light and radio timers, leave shades and curtains in normal positions and stop mail and newspaper deliveries.

When you travel:
Use credit cards and travelers' checks.
Take as little cash and few credit cards as possible.

Keep valuables close to you.
Don't dangle a purse by the straps. Carry a wallet in a front pant or coat pocket, or use a money pouch.

Always keep your belongings under your control.
Don't leave them where someone could easily pick them up.

Stay alert.
Don't look confused or lost. Be on guard for pickpockets and for staged mishaps, like someone bumping into you or spilling a drink.

Don't draw attention to yourself.
Displaying cash or valuables is an open invitation to thieves.

Identify your property.
Put your driver's license number and state on your property. Use an indelible marker or an engraving tool.

Once you arrive:
Keep your luggage locked.
Make sure it's under your control at all times.

Protect your valuables.
Keep them in a hotel safe or safe deposit box.

Check the neighborhood.
Ask the hotel staff about local conditions.

Check the locks in your room.
Expect deadbolts and peepholes. Use all the locks. Coded electronic entry cards are safer than key locks.

Verify visitors before opening the door.
If a person claims to be a hotel employee, call the front desk to make sure the person is supposed to be there before opening the door.

Avoid displaying your room keys.
Guard against leaving them in public places, like at the swimming pool or at a restaurant table.

Report suspicious activity.
Call the hotel staff. If you think it's an emergency, call 911 or the local emergency number.

CAR SECURITY

Every 19 seconds, one vehicle is stolen in the U.S.

Where? Just about anywhere. In big cities and small towns, in malls, streets, driveways, parking lots, car dealerships—even closed garages.

When? Just about anytime, although many carjackings happen during late-night hours.

Why? There are several reasons given for car theft:

— It's a crime of opportunity. Cars are easy to steal.

— For some young people, carjacking may be a rite of passage or a thrill.

— Cars provide quick cash for drug users and others.

Car theft poses more than just an economic hardship for the victims. It increases everyone's insurance premiums and may lead to other, violent crimes.

This section gives you tips on how to prevent car-linked crime from happening to you. But remember, nothing is 100 percent effective.

◆

Reduce Your Risk

Park in well-lighted, busy areas.

Park near sidewalks or walkways. Avoid dumpsters, woods, large vans or anything else that limits your visibility.

Always lock your car.

Whether you're in the car or not, it's important that all doors be locked. And roll your windows all the way up.

Put valuables in the trunk.

Even if the car is locked, don't leave valuables in plain view.

Never leave your car running.

And never leave the keys in your car.

Give the attendant only your ignition key.

If you're parking in a commercial garage or lot, just your ignition key should be given to the attendant. Make sure your name and home address are not attached.

Take your registration and insurance card with you.

Don't leave personal identification documents or credit cards in your vehicle.

Copy your VIN.
Keep a copy of your vehicle identification number with your driver's license.

Etch your VIN.
Etch your vehicle registration number on your vehicle's windows, doors, fenders and trunk lid. It deters thieves, who have to remove or replace the etched parts before selling the car.

Install a steering wheel lock.
Commonly called clubs, collars or j-bars, these mechanical devices lock to the steering wheel, column or brake and prevent the wheel from being turned.

Getting into Your Vehicle

Stay alert.
Walk with purpose.

Have your key in hand.
Look around and inside your car before you get in.

Trust your instincts.
If something—or someone—makes you nervous, get into the car quickly, lock the doors and drive away.

CAR SECURITY

On the Road

Keep doors locked and windows up.
Even if it's hot and you don't have air conditioning, keep the windows at least partially rolled up.

Leave room to maneuver.
When you're coming to a stop, leave room to get around other cars if you sense trouble.

Drive in the center lane.
It makes it harder for would-be carjackers to approach the car.

Avoid driving alone.
Go with someone else if you can, especially at night.

Keep valuables out of sight.
Put purses, briefcases and other valuables either in the trunk or on the passenger floor space—away from where a thief might grab them.

Avoid stopping to help strangers.
If someone you don't know has car problems, drive to the nearest phone and call police to help.

Keep your car in good shape.
Make sure there's enough gas to get there and back. Check fluids, belts and tires periodically.

Don't pick up hitchhikers.
And don't be a hitchhiker.

Consider a CB radio or cellular phone.
It makes it easier to summon help.

If You're Carjacked

Don't struggle with a carjacker.
Give up your car. Don't argue. Your life is more important than a car.

Leave the area quickly.
And report the incident to the police.

Remember details.
Try to relate to police what the carjacker looked like— race, sex, age, hair and eye color, clothes, etc.

Take Action

Get the word out.
Work with Neighborhood Watch groups and others to prevent carjacking. Try community forums, posters, etc.

Make sure teens get the word.
Encourage driver education classes to talk with teens about the issue.

Air tips.
Ask local radio stations to air carjacking prevention tips during commuting hours.

Send tips.
Ask car insurance agents to include carjacking prevention tips with premium notices.

Distribute tips.
Place prevention fliers or brochures in the waiting rooms of car dealerships, repair shops and gas stations.

Don't Get Caught in the "Bump and Rob"

1. A car, usually with at least one passenger in it, bumps you in traffic.

2. You quickly get out to check damage and exchange information.

3. The other driver, or a passenger, jumps in your car and drives off.

If you're bumped by another car, look around before you get out. Make sure there are other cars around. Look at the car that bumped you.

If the situation makes you nervous, memorize or jot down the car's license plate; signal the other car to follow you. Drive to the nearest police station or busy, well-lighted area.

If you do get out of your car, take your keys with you. Stay alert.

WHAT TO TEACH KIDS

More than 5,000 children are victims of violent crime in the country each day. Murder. Rape. Robbery. Or assault.

These numbers are frightening. But the situation does not have to continue. People are turning the tables on crime, creating safer neighborhoods, safer schools, safer environments.

There are many ways to help prevent crime. Some can be done right now. Others take time. Some require help from others. Others don't. Most require little or no money.

This section talks about what you can teach kids to help prevent crime—and what you and your neighbors can do to keep crime away from kids.

◆

Things Kids Can Do

Settle arguments with words, not fists.
And don't stand around watching others argue. That's how crowds form, which could encourage violence.

Never carry a gun or other weapon.
It's against the law and a sure way to turn a simple argument into something much worse.

Take a friend along.
Whether you're playing, walking or biking, don't go it alone. And always let a responsible adult know where you are.

Learn safe routes and places to get help.
Find out where it's safest to walk in the neighborhood. If you sense danger, get out and alert an adult.

Avoid strangers.
Don't open the door or go anywhere with someone you and your parents don't know and trust.

Get away from bad situations.
If someone tries to abuse you, say no, get away and tell a trusted adult.

Report crime.
If you see something suspicious, report it to police, school authorities or parents.

Don't use alcohol or other drugs.
Stay away from places and people associated with them.

Stick with friends who are against violence and drugs.

And stay away from known trouble spots.

Get involved with school projects.

Especially those that make your school safer and better. Anti-drug rallies and poster contests against violence are examples.

Set an example for younger kids.

Volunteer to help with community efforts to stop crime.

Things Adults Can Do

Stay informed about your kids.
Insist that you always know where your kids are, what they're doing and who they are with.

Get involved.
Help with community and neighborhood anti-crime and community improvement efforts.

Stand up to crime.
Report suspicious activity. Agree to testify when necessary.

Know your neighbors.
Agree to look out for each other. Get organized; work with police.

Settle arguments without violence.
Be a good role model for your kids.

Don't carry a weapon.
You lose, whether you use it or it's used on you.

Don't support illegal activities.
Buying stolen property or using illegal drugs sends the wrong message to a child.

Volunteer your home.
Offer it as a reliable source of help for kids who are scared or need assistance.

Things You and Your Neighbors Can Do

Find positive activities for kids.

Make sure neighborhood youth have constructive things to do in their spare time. That could include organized basketball or baseball leagues, tutoring programs, part-time work and volunteer activities.

Set up a Neighborhood Watch.

Work with police to organize a community patrol or similar effort.

Build a partnership with police.

Focus on solving problems, not on reacting to crises.

Focus on "safety in numbers."

Hold anti-crime rallies, marches or other group activities.

Clean up the neighborhood.

Get everyone involved. Call the city public works department and ask for help in cleaning up.

Ask officials for help.

If criminals are in your neighborhood or building, ask city officials to help in enforcing anti-noise laws, housing codes, health and fire codes, drug-free clauses in rental leases, etc.

Form a Court Watch.

It will help support victims and witnesses to see that criminals get fairly punished.

Develop an anti-crime phone list.

It's a list of organizations that provide counseling, job training and other services. Share the list with neighbors.

How You Can Help Prevent Gangs

There are many kinds of gangs. And they are found in all kinds of communities—big and small. Whatever type your community is facing, gangs spell trouble. They bring fear and violence to a neighborhood.

There's a lot parents can do to prevent your own children from joining gangs.

Learn signs of gang activity.
Examples include graffiti with special lettering, unique clothing or ways of wearing clothes, special hand signals, coded language and tattoos.

Learn why youth join gangs.
Reasons given include excitement, recognition, protection, intimidation from other youth, access to money, to be with friends, a sense of belonging, and lack of alternatives.

Use your parenting skills.
Make sure you talk—really talk—with your children. And listen, too.

Get involved with positive alternatives.
Make sure youth have healthy outlets, like sports, hobbies, youth clubs, etc.

Build partnerships with others.
Work with government agencies, schools, civic groups and religious organizations to educate the community about gangs and anti-gang efforts.

TAKE BACK YOUR NEIGHBORHOOD
Starting a Neighborhood Watch Program

Something may be wrong in your neighborhood. Perhaps violence is increasing. Maybe a child was robbed. A car was stolen. Some homes were burglarized. Or graffiti is showing up.

Things might be quiet right now, but you can see the early warning signs. The neighborhood needs help. The trick is to act right now to prevent the problem from growing.

Neighborhood Watch, Block Watch, Crime Watch—whatever it's called—is one of the most effective and inexpensive answers to crime.

Neighbor Watch is an association of neighbors who look out for each other's families and property. They alert police to suspicious activity and work together to make their community a safer place to live.

This section tells you how to start one—and what a Neighborhood Watch program can and should do.

◆

TAKE BACK YOUR NEIGHBORHOOD

First off, don't be afraid.

When people see violence happening around them, they tend to shy away from stepping forward to act. Fear of revenge is a common reaction. There are ways to counter that fear.

Simply joining together helps.
There's strength in numbers. Criminals attack lone victims, not groups. And groups can form rallies to demonstrate their strength.

Work with police.
Set up a system that lets people report crime to police anonymously.

Meet away from the problem.
Groups can meet several blocks away, at a local church, school or other building.

Get Started

Find out what's going on.
See if another group is already working on preventing crime and can help you get started.

Recruit likely groups.
Is there an existing group that ought to be involved in preventing crime? A PTA, Lion's Club or other group may be a base for action.

Start your own group.
If you can't find an existing group to help, start your own. You don't have to be a leader, but you could conduct the first meeting.

Get Neighbors Together

Set a date, time and place.
Make sure it doesn't interfere with other important events. Publicize the meeting at least one week in advance.

Invite the neighbors.
The invitation could be by phone, by flier, knocking on doors—or just talking over the back fence.

Ask local officials to attend.
Police or sheriff officials will send someone to the meeting to explain how they can help. They'll help train members in home security, reporting skills and information on local crime patterns.

Invite young people.
In they're part of the problem, they should be part of the solution.

Draw up an agenda.
Keep the first meeting fairly brief— no more than 2 hours.

Share the work.
It gets people working together from the start. One person could take meeting notes, another could lead discussion, and so on.

Focus on action.
Allow people to share concerns, but don't let the meeting turn into a gripe session. Make sure clear decisions are made.

Start with short-term goals.
Decide what topics take top priority (drugs, vandalism, etc.). Then, discuss realistic solutions, develop short- and long-term goals and take action.

Select a coordinator and block captains.
These people are responsible for organizing meetings and relaying information to members.

Put up signs.
Work with local officials to put up Neighborhood Watch signs. Usually, these signs are put up after at least 50 percent of the households are enrolled.

What Neighbors Should Look For

— Someone screaming or calling for help.

— Someone looking into windows and parked cars.

— Unusual noises.

— Property being taken out of houses where no one is home, or out of closed businesses.

— Vehicles moving slowly with no apparent destination, or with lights out.

— Anyone being forced into a vehicle.

— A stranger sitting in a car or talking to a child.

— Abandoned cars.

— Report these incidents promptly to the police or sheriff's department.

Tips for Success

Keep it simple.
Take the obvious route to solve problems. If graffiti's a concern, for example, just paint over it, with permission from the property owners.

Get everyone into the act.
People will do things if asked. Canvass door-to-door to recruit members.

Start with success.
A small success—quickly reachable—boosts enthusiasm.

Follow through.
If you say there will be a meeting, make sure there is one. If you announce a rally, hold it.

Get endorsed by the police or sheriff's department.
They are sources of information on home security, crime patterns and crime reporting methods.

Establish a telephone tree.
It gets information out quickly. Try electronic bulletin boards, too.

Divide up the work.
Leaders can burn out. Switch off responsibilities.

Keep in touch—often.

Newsletters, special events, fliers, phone calls—they all help keep people informed and interested. Make sure the information you share is accurate.

Choose activities people are comfortable doing.

Make the most of local talent and their willingness to participate.

Try Some of These Ideas for Your Neighborhood Watch

— Ask police for help in forming a citizen patrol that walks or drives through the neighborhood, writing down license plate numbers and descriptions of suspicious people.

— Demonstrate against landlords who rent property to known drug dealers.

— Organize neighborhood clean-up campaigns.

— March or organize a vigil to demonstrate the neighborhood's will to drive out crime.

— Make sure the media covers these events. Let everyone know that neighbors and police care and are taking action.

— Videotape or photograph suspicious activity from a safe place. Give the information to police.

SPECIAL CRIME PREVENTION STEPS IN RURAL AREAS

Much of the information found throughout this booklet applies both to urban and rural areas. There are some crime problems, however, that are unique to rural communities.

Vandals can destroy crops and fields. Thieves can steal farm equipment and livestock.

Investing some time and money now means better security around your property, and less worry about crime and your family's security.

This section lists some of the steps you can take to safeguard your rural environment.

◆

SPECIAL CRIME PREVENTION STEPS IN RURAL AREAS

Check the Outside

Keep all areas well-lighted.

This includes your house, driveway, barns and other buildings. Use timers that automatically turn on outside lights when it gets dark.

Keep fences in good shape.

Make sure access roads have gates or cables stretched between posts cemented in the ground. Make them visible with flags or streamers.

Put up signs.

Warn potential intruders by putting up "No Trespassing," "No Hunting" or other appropriate signs around your property.

Protect Your Equipment

Don't leave major equipment in fields overnight.

Lock it in a barn or shed near the house, or park it near your house or a neighbor's. If machines must be left outside, disable them by removing the rotor, distributor or battery.

Use padlocks or deadbolts.

Secure gas pumps, gas tanks, storage bins and grain elevators with padlocks or deadbolts. Keep small equipment locked away.

Keep keys away.

Don't leave them in vehicles or farm equipment.

Put away tools.

Don't leave them in the open back of a pick-up truck or in an unsecured truck bed toolbox.

Guard Your Property

Use a personal ID number.
A driver's license marked on tools, guns and equipment can cut crime.

Mark livestock.
The best way is through tattoos (usually on the ear.) Eartags and neckchains can be removed.

Record valuable timber.
Use a paint stripe on each tree.

Check employee references.
Before they start, talk to them about your crime prevention measures.

Be A Good Neighbor

Get together with others in the community to start a Farm Watch group. Involve all ages and work with law enforcement officials. You can recruit people from church and civic groups.

CB radios or cellular phones can be used to report suspicious activity to the sheriff's department.

Ask neighbors to check your property. Return the favor when they leave on business or vacation trips.

HOW TO IDENTIFY LOCAL RESOURCES

Crime Prevention Check

Your local police or sheriff's department may have a prevention specialist who can inspect your property with you, pointing out specific steps you can take to better secure your property. Check your local phone directory.

The telephone number to call is

_____

Reporting Crime

In cities, report crime to the local police. In rural areas, small towns or outlying suburban areas, call the sheriff's department to report a crime.

The telephone number to call is

_____

Victim Assistance

Cities and towns may have a number of resources to help
victims of crime. Check your local phone directory for
resources available in your community.

District Attorney's Office

_____

District Attorney's Victim Assistance Office

_____

Crisis Counseling Center

_____

Mental Health Center Crisis Service

_____

Rape Crisis Center

_____

Women's Health Crisis Center

_____

General Information

Many libraries and schools keep a file of information about resources in the community pertaining to crime. Check with your library or school. List below any additional resources they provide.

_____

_____

_____

_____

_____

_____

_____

_____

For additional information, contact:

National Crime Prevention Council
1700 K Street, NW, Second Floor
Washington, D.C. 20006-3817
202-466-6272